Beyond the GPA

How to Give Your Student an Edge With College Admissions

Susie Watts

Book Cover and Formatting provided by Trisha Fuentes

Contents

Introduction

"Beyond the GPA: How to Give Your Student an Edge with College Admissions" is a comprehensive guide to navigating the college planning process. From researching colleges to showcasing a student's extracurricular activities and crafting a compelling personal statement, everything you need to know is here. Throughout the book, readers will find valuable step-by-step strategies, helpful FYIs and expert tips that offer additional guidance by diving deep into relevant topics.

Drawing on 30 years of experience as a college consultant, I have provided suggestions to help students increase their chances of acceptance to the schools they would like to attend. Whether your child is a straight-A student or just working hard to maintain grades, this book will maximize your teen's chances for success. Parents will learn how to leverage their child's unique strengths and address their weaknesses, ultimately helping them stand out in a competitive field of applicants.

With "Beyond the GPA: How to Give Your Student an Edge with College Admissions" as your guide, you'll be well on your way to helping your student get into the right colleges, the ones that fit academically, personally, and financially. These are the schools where students will be happy and thrive!

Let's get started...

Strategy 1

Mapping Your Future: Freshmen, Sophomores, First Semester Juniors

A successful high school experience is integral to preparing for college admission. Here are some tips to help students get off on the right start.

AS A FRESHMAN

Set Goals: Work with students to set academic and extracurricular goals for the year. Establishing a four-year plan will enable them to stay focused and motivated throughout high school. Students should meet with their high school counselor at the beginning of their freshman year to discuss their classes and how they align with their future goals.

Get Involved: Encourage students to join activities outside of the classroom. These can include sports, clubs, volunteering, or individual pursuits. These activities will help them explore their interests, develop unique skills, and meet new people. Extracurriculars will also show colleges that students enjoy participating in high school activities and are engaged in their community.

Develop Study Skills: Help students find ways to stay organized, manage their time, and seek help, if needed. Students should learn the importance of taking notes and reviewing them every night. They should also create a schedule for assignments, tests, activities, and scheduled appointments. Consider something like Schooltraq as an academic planner.

Encourage Reading: Expose students to books, newspapers, and magazines that align with their interests. Reading increases vocabulary and improves comprehension skills. It also helps reduce stress in students.

Improve Vocabulary: Improving vocabulary enhances students' communication skills, allowing them to express themselves effectively in written and spoken forms. It also improves their comprehension and critical thinking skills.

Consider A College Savings Plan: Look into a 529 program or consider increasing your contribution to an existing one if you have already started one.

AS A SOPHOMORE

Review Your Courses: Encourage students to take a few challenging classes that will prepare them for honors, AP, or dual-enrollment courses. Colleges love to see academic rigor in a potential student's schedule.

Continue to Work on Study Skills and Grades: Discuss with your child the significance of good grades. While the GPA isn't everything, students should understand the power of their transcript for college admission. Many admission officers believe that good grades in high school predict academic success, retention, and graduation rates in college.

Stay Involved with Extracurricular Activities: Colleges like to see that students can manage their time between extracurriculars and their schoolwork. They also would rather see genuine involvement in one or two activities than minimal involvement in many.

Speak with High School Counselor: Suggest students speak with their school counselor about when they should take the Pre-ACT. Many schools allow 10th graders to take the PSAT. Students can also discuss what they can do to prepare for the next year or two and, eventually, college.

Discuss Summer Plans: Colleges want to see students expand their interests over the summer. Whether pursuing a summer job, volunteering in the community, or getting involved in a particular project, colleges like to see productive students. Early planning will ensure that opportunities are available.

Plan Financially: If your child is a sophomore, it's important to note that the base tax year for financial aid is this year. You have until the end of this year to implement any tax or financial strategies that may increase your aid eligibility when you fill out the Free Application for Federal Student Aid (FAFSA) in your student's senior year.

AS A 1st SEMESTER JUNIOR

Focus on Academics: A student's junior transcript is the last year of grades for colleges to look at as they consider applicants for admission. Students need to continue to work hard and take their classes seriously. Those with mediocre grades must show an upward trend towards improving their overall GPA. Good grades indicate to colleges that students can and want to succeed.

Visit Local Colleges: Get a feel for the school setting. Students can see the campus layout, explore the buildings and facilities, and familiarize themselves with the atmosphere and surrounding community. A college visit can determine what kind of school would be a good fit for them.

Be Selective with Extracurricular Activities: If students have developed a passion for one or two of their extracurriculars, help them look for ways to get further involved or take on some leadership responsibility. Some students may also want to choose a project involving one of their activities. For example: If your teen likes reading, why not have them volunteer to teach children how to read? If they play a sport, encourage them to become a coach or referee for a team of younger players. If students love science, suggest they follow up with a STEM project they create and research independently.

Get to Know Teachers: High school juniors need to establish a relationship with a teacher or two and get to know them more personally. Students should participate in class and ask questions. They should also attend study sessions and meet with teachers during a free period. If students want a good recommendation from a teacher for college, they need to find time to connect.

Attend College Fairs: Students should attend college fairs whenever they are available. These events allow them to learn about different colleges and universities, speak with admissions representatives, and gather information about the admissions process.

Student Checklist

1. Did you set up a four-year plan?
2. What steps did you take to get organized?
3. In what extracurricular activities are you participating?
4. Do you need help with any of your classes?
5. What have you read recently?

6. What are your plans for the summer?
7. What teachers did you meet with?

Fun Idea:

Sit down with your teen and watch movies that take place on college campuses, such as "Legally Blonde," "Good Will Hunting," or "The Social Network." These movies can give students a glimpse into college life and inspire them to start their college planning.

Strategy 2

The Power of Asking Questions: What Are Your Student's College Priorities?

Find a time when you and your teen can sit down and discuss what factors are important for them in a college experience. By understanding your child's goals, interests, and values, you can provide guidance and support in selecting the best schools for your child. Remember that your student may want different things from their college experience than you do. Hopefully, this conversation will encourage open communication and trust between you and your student, enabling you to work together as a team throughout the college planning process.

TIPS - Beginning the Conversation

- Help students discover who they are.
- Let students take the lead.
- Don't let college costs limit your school choices.
- College websites are your most reliable resource for information.
- While it is sometimes helpful to gain insights from other parents, every student's situation and needs are unique, and what works for one family may not work for another. Don't believe everything you hear!

- Have your student explore a variety of colleges and universities, including those they may have yet to discover or those with which parents are not familiar.
- Encourage your student to communicate their thoughts and preferences about different college. Listen carefully to their input. Ask questions and be engaged in the process with them.
- Talk to students about the cost of tuition, room and board, and other expenses. Explore options for financial aid and scholarships.
- Look at the academic programs offered at different colleges to ensure they align with your student's interests and career goals. Look into each school's faculty, course offerings, and research opportunities.
- Respect your high school counselor. Attend presentations given by the school.

College Planning Questions to Ask Your Teen

Reasons for going to college

- Why do you want to go to college?
- Is it necessary for your friends to recognize the college you are attending?

Learning preferences

- What kind of learning environment do you like? Discussion, lectures, hands-on?
- What do you think about the size of a school? Would you like one that is small, medium, or large? Help students understand size by comparing colleges to schools they may already know.

- Have you considered what you want to study in college? Knowing their intended major can help narrow the list of schools to consider. No problem if your student has no idea.
- Have you considered what kind of school you want to attend (e.g., public vs. private, urban vs. rural, outdoorsy vs. more metropolitan, etc.?) This will help you understand what kind of environment your student may prefer.
- Have you considered the location of the school? Talk about geographic areas like the northwest, south, mid-Atlantic, etc. Location can be important for factors such as cost of living, internship opportunities, weather, and access to cultural and recreational activities.

Personal characteristics and interests

- Give me three adjectives that your friends would use to describe you.
- What do you like to do when you're not attending classes?
- What classes have you enjoyed the most and why?
- What will you contribute to a college?
- What aspect of college life are you most excited about?

High school and college comparison

- In what ways do you want your college to be like your high school?
- In what ways do you want it to be different?

Future Goals

- What would you like to learn more about?
- How much academic challenge do you want?
- What are three experiences you want to have in college?

- Is there any aspect of your transcript or overall application that might need an explanation?

Standardized Tests

- What do you know about the SAT and ACT?
- Do you know which test is given at your school?

FYI - The SAT and ACT

- The SAT and ACT are standardized tests some colleges and universities use for admissions. While both tests assess a student's knowledge and skills in English, math, and reading, there are some differences. Below is a brief description of each.
- **The SAT (Scholastic Assessment Test)**

  The College Board offers the SAT, which is a 3-hour test. The digital SAT is 2 hours and 14 minutes. The SAT has two main sections: Evidence-Based reading and writing and math. The Evidence-Based reading and writing section includes reading, writing and language questions. The math section includes multiple-choice and grid-in questions, testing students on algebra, geometry, and trigonometry.
- **The ACT (American College Test)**

  ACT, Inc. offers the ACT, a 2-hour and 55-minute test. It has four main sections: English, math, reading, and science. The English section includes questions on grammar, punctuation, and usage. The math section covers topics such as algebra, geometry, and trigonometry. The reading section includes passages and questions testing comprehension skills. Finally, the science section focuses on interpreting data and graphs.
- Both tests are scored on a scale: 400-1600 (SAT) and 1-36 (ACT), with no penalty for guessing. Most colleges accept the SAT or ACT,

and many students take both tests to determine which one they perform better on.

- Superscoring is a practice used by some colleges and universities. Instead of looking at a student's highest score on a single SAT or ACT, a school will combine the highest section scores from multiple tests to create a new composite score. For example, if a student takes the SAT twice and scores 600 on the math section the first time and 650 on the reading section the second time, a college that superstores would consider the student's composite score to be 1250 rather than just the highest score from a single test. Check with each school where the student is applying to find out whether they superstore on the SAT and ACT.

TIPS - To Prepare for the SAT and ACT

- **Prepare For The Tests:** Giving your student ample time to prepare for the SAT or ACT is essential. Your child should start studying a few months before the tests are scheduled.
- **Practice On Actual Tests:** Real tests are an excellent way for students to become familiar with the format and content of the SAT or ACT. Please encourage your child to take several practice tests and review their results to identify challenging areas.
- **Understand The Test Formats:** The SAT and ACT have different formats, so it's essential for your student to understand the structure of each test. Have your child review the format and timing of the test to ensure they are confident with it on test day.
- **Take A Test Prep Class Or Consider A Tutor:** Many reasonably priced courses will help your child prepare for these two tests. A tutor offers personalized instruction and help students focus on their areas of weakness.

- **Register In January Of Junior Year To Take Both Tests:** Some high schools have all juniors take the SAT or ACT in school. You do not need to register for this. Register for the test that is not given at the school.

FYI - Applying Test-Optional

- Test-optional colleges do not require applicants to submit standardized test scores (such as the SAT or ACT) as part of the admissions process.
- Applying to colleges test-optional has both advantages and disadvantages. The primary benefit is that it allows students who do not excel in standardized testing to demonstrate their strengths and talents through other means, such as their GPA, extracurricular activities, essays, and recommendation letters.
- On the other hand, with test scores, it may be easier for a college to accurately assess students academic abilities and determine whether they are a good fit for their school. Grading systems and high school courses differ significantly from one school to another. Sometimes submitting test scores is the only standardized measure colleges have to evaluate applicants.
- Many colleges and universities use test scores to award merit-based scholarships or for honors programs. These scholarships are awarded to students based on their academic achievements rather than financial need. Understand that test optional is NOT test blind, and if, two college applicants appear equal, but one turns in test scores and the other does not, the applicant with test scores will most likely get in and receive more merit money. In other words, test scores can be a bonus!
- It is always a good idea to research the specific policies and requirements of the colleges you are considering to make sure you are making the right decision regarding test scores.

Student Checklist

1. What are you doing to prepare for the SAT and ACT?
2. Do you have dates on the calendar when you will be taking the tests?
3. What test-taking strategies would be most helpful for you to learn? (Time management, increasing reading speed, how to guess, etc.)

Strategy 3

Researching Schools: Navigating the College Search

You and your student should research colleges that align with their academic and personal interests, career goals, and financial situation. Thorough research can help students understand each college's admission requirements, acceptance rates, and selectivity, allowing them to choose realistic options.

Researching schools can also help students discover "hidden gem colleges" that they may not have considered before. Building a well-rounded college list with a range of options can increase the chances of finding the best-fit schools to ensure that your student has good choices to make a final decision.

Getting Started:

Create A Professional Email Account: It should include your student's first and last name. Avoid nicknames or any overly complicated text. Your student can use this new email account exclusively for their college search and admissions communications. Gmail is a great option that is free and easy to set up.

It's beneficial to consolidate all communications with colleges within a single account, avoiding messages getting lost in their other email accounts. Students should not use a school account for their college admissions communications.

Return To Your Student's List Of Priorities: Does your student value academic reputation, location, size, cost, campus life, or something else? Big Future at the College Board and College Express are a few great websites to begin the search.

Visit College Websites: Check out each school's academics, campus life, student profile, admission requirements, and whatever else interests them. This will give your student an idea of the college's programs and activities. Students should also request undergraduate information from each school or join the mailing list on their websites.

Create A College Search Spreadsheet: Fill in the college spreadsheet with the school name, location, number of undergraduate students, acceptance rate, average GPA, number of students returning from their freshman to sophomore year, academic calendar, students in housing, and how many graduate in four years. You can find all of the information on the College Data website.

Use Online Resources: College Navigator is a database maintained by the National Center for Education Statistics to compare colleges and learn more about each program, costs, and graduation rates. Students should also check out websites for The Colleges that Change Lives and Colleges of Distinction. Both websites offer schools that are worth considering!

Meet College Representatives: Every fall, college representatives visit local high schools to meet students who might be interested in their universities. Your student should find out who will be coming to their school and plan to attend the presentation and meet the representatives.

One Book To Purchase: The Fiske Guide to Colleges is a reputable source of information that offers independent reviews and assessments of over 300 schools. It also includes student feedback and perspectives, providing a well-rounded view of campus life and culture.

Look For Online College Reviews: Niche and Unigo provide student reviews to research and compare colleges, read reviews from current and former students and gain insights into the admissions process.

Consider Tuition Saving Programs: These programs are for students in the United States.

- **WUE (Western Undergraduate Exchange):** A regional tuition-reciprocity program in the western United States. It allows students who are residents of WUE-participating states to enroll in participating colleges and universities in other states at reduced tuition rates. Under WUE, students typically pay 150% of the in-state tuition rate, which is significantly lower than the out-of-state tuition.
- **WICHE (Western Interstate Commission for Higher Education):** An organization that coordinates various higher education initiatives among its member states in the western United States. WICHE operates multiple programs, including the WUE program mentioned above.
- **NEBHE (New England Board of Higher Education):** Offers the New England Regional Student Program (RSP), which allows New England residents to enroll in out-of-state public colleges and universities in the region at discounted tuition rates for certain programs not available in their home state.
- **MSEP (Midwest Student Exchange Program):** Enables students from participating Midwestern states to attend public colleges and universities in other participating states at reduced tuition rates. This program aims to expand educational opportunities within the Midwest region.

- **Academic Common Market:** Operated by the Southern Regional Education Board (SREB), allows students to access out-of-state college programs at in-state tuition rates. It is available for specific undergraduate and graduate programs not offered in their home state within the Southern region.

These programs are intended to make higher education more affordable and accessible for students, particularly when pursuing programs that may not be available or have limited capacity in their home states. It's important to note that each program has specific eligibility criteria and application processes, so students should research and review the requirements of the program they are interested in before applying.

FYI - The NET Price Calculator

- To use a net price calculator, you must typically provide information about your financial situation, such as your family's income and assets. The calculator will then use this, along with information about the cost of tuition, fees, and other expenses at the college, to estimate the total cost of attending the school and the amount of financial aid you may be eligible to receive.
- The net price calculator on college websites is extremely helpful for estimating the actual cost of attendance, including tuition, fees, and room and board, after considering financial aid and scholarships. This will help you make informed decisions about college afford-ability.
- College net price calculators can be a helpful tool for students and their families as they plan for college and compare the costs of different colleges. However, it's important to note that the estimates provided by these calculators are only estimates. The actual cost of attending a college may differ based on your circumstances and the financial aid you receive.

TIPS

- The net price calculator should be on the financial aid page on every college website.
- The net price calculator can give you an idea of the loans, scholarships, and grants you may get from a specific school.
- It's important to note that net price calculators are a reference point. They are not always accurate, nor do they guarantee financial aid.

Student Checklist

1. Which colleges do you want to explore further?
2. Did the net price calculator provide a useful estimate for you to consider in your college assessment?
3. Which colleges have emailed you, and what have they sent?

Strategy 4

Choosing a Major: Passion vs. Practicality

When applying to college, some students have a particular major in mind. However, it is common for students to also apply as undecided. This can be a smart decision as it allows them to explore their interests and passions while providing flexibility in their academic courses. Applying undecided also means that students can consider a range of majors and programs and find a major they had not considered before.

Students can use a few strategies to help them find a college major:

Explore Interests and Strengths: Help your student to think about the subjects they have enjoyed learning, and try to find a major that aligns with those interests. This can help make their studies more enjoyable and rewarding.

Consider Career Goals: Assist your student in researching different career paths to see which majors are most relevant to the work they want to do.

Explore College Websites: Many colleges and universities have websites about their academic programs, including descriptions of different majors and career paths.

Online College Major and Career Search Tools: Several websites help students determine which unique personality traits might lead to a potential major. Some websites allow students to search for colleges based on specific criteria, including different majors. Career Explorer, My Next Move, and My Majors are websites to explore.

Professional Associations: Professional associations in various industries often have resources for students interested in pursuing careers in those fields. For example, the American Medical Association has a website with information about careers in healthcare. The American Bar Association has resources for students interested in law. By using these resources, students can explore different college majors and career options.

TIPS

- Don't be afraid if your student changes their mind. It's okay to start college thinking about a major in one subject and then going in a different direction. Many students do this, and it's a normal part of finding the right major.
- Your student should talk with colleges to determine how easy it is to change a major. Some schools make it very difficult, whereas it is relatively common at other colleges.
- Your student should not choose a major because they think getting accepted to a university will be easier than with a more competitive major.
- Discuss and evaluate schools with your child, looking at potential majors and career paths.

FYI - Creating a High School Resume

A high school resume summarizes your student's education, extracurricular activities, and relevant experiences. A well-crafted resume can help students stand out from other applicants and give them a competitive edge when applying to college, for scholarships, internships, or summer jobs.

Include The Following Information:

Personal Information: Your formal name, home address, cell phone number, and email address.

Academics: List your high school, location, GPA, and graduation date.

Work Experience: Any employment, including temporary work and summer jobs. List the job title, company, dates, and responsibilities. (Start with the most recent)

Activities And Volunteer Work: List any extracurricular activities, such as sports, clubs, or volunteer work. Include the activity name, dates of participation, and your role in the activity or volunteer work. (Start with the most recent and those with the biggest time commitment)

Skills: Include relevant skills, such as proficiency in a software program or foreign language. You can also mention soft skills such as communication, problem-solving, and teamwork.

Awards and Achievements: Include any awards or honors you have received, such as academic awards or scholarships.

TIPS

- Remind your student to customize their resume to highlight their unique skills and experiences. They should proofread it carefully for content, spelling, and grammar errors.
- If a college application has a place where students can upload a resume, they should do it!

Student Checklist

1. What classes do you find most interesting?
2. What would you like to be doing in ten years for a career?
3. Did you take one of the personality tests? What did it reveal about you?
4. If you were guaranteed success, what career would you choose?

Strategy 5

Extracurricular and Summer Activities: The Power of Getting Involved

Colleges typically look for extracurriculars demonstrating a student's dedication, leadership skills, and interests. These can include participation in any activities outside of the classroom.

Colleges want to see that students have taken the initiative to pursue their interests and have made an effort to contribute to their community. They may also look for activities that require a significant time commitment or a leadership role.

In addition, colleges may look for extracurriculars that align with the values and mission of the school. For example, a college emphasizing sustainability may be interested in applicants participating in environmental advocacy groups or conservation efforts.

FYI - Suggested Extracurricular Activities

- Actively participate in a youth or faith-based organization.
- Get involved in student government.

- Plan and execute a project. What could you do to improve your community or school?
- Engage in creative endeavors: Art, music, theater, photography, etc.
- Start a petition for change.
- Pursue a hobby: Stamp collecting, cooking, investing, or thrifting.
- Join a sports team

TIPS

- The college application must show that your student is more than their academic studies.
- Colleges also want to know what students will contribute to their campus.
- Colleges are far more interested in the depth a student has with an activity than they are with a long list that shows no long-term commitment.

FYI - Ideas for Summer Activities

- Students need to have fun in the summer for their mental and emotional health, but they can have fun while being productive. Summer pursuits for high school students are essential for college admission because they can show that they are motivated, curious, and responsible. They can also provide opportunities for students to develop valuable skills, such as teamwork, leadership, and communication. So what can teenagers do? Check out some options below.
- **Volunteer Work:** Community service can include helping at a local food bank, tutoring younger students, teaching computer skills to senior citizens, walking dogs at an animal shelter, or volunteering at a museum or library.

- **Apply For An Internship:** Students can gain valuable experience and insight into a particular career or industry through an internship. Many colleges like to see students who have taken the initiative to pursue an internship in a field of interest. Finding something may require cold-calling or cold-emailing, but it is worth the effort. Try this site for internships: SPARK Summer Internship Program.
- **Attend A Summer Program:** High school students can attend summer programs that provide academic enrichment, leadership development, or cultural immersion opportunities. These programs can demonstrate a student's intellectual curiosity; however, colleges often refer to them as pay-to-play because most require money to participate. Whether or not it's worth it is up to your family. These programs will not help a student gain admission to a particular college.
- **Look Into A Research Project:** Many colleges are interested in students who have engaged in independent research projects or have worked with faculty members on research initiatives. Students can email professors at universities to see whether they have a project that could use an assistant. If not, students can always do research on their own, which will demonstrate to colleges their ability to work independently.
- **Start A Small Business Or Get A Job:** Starting a small business or creating a service can demonstrate a student's creativity, initiative, and problem-solving skills. Your teen can also offer house sitting, dog walking, lawn and garden care, and other services.
- **Begin A New Hobby:** The summer is an excellent time for your student to discover a new hobby or pursue one they already have. Colleges are looking for students with different interests.
- **Take A Course:** Find a course online that interests you, and sign up. Colleges offer many classes online, often for free.

TIPS

- Don't wait until May for your child to make summer plans.
- Encourage students to read books they did not have time to read during the school year.
- Make sure your child has free time to enjoy the summer.

Student Checklist

1. What extracurricular activities do you enjoy the most?
2. What opportunities do you have to show leadership experience?
3. What are your plans for the summer?

Strategy 6

Senior Year Classes: Charting Your Course

Selecting senior-year courses is an important decision that can impact your student's future college opportunities. Your teen must consider their strengths, interests, and future goals when choosing their courses.

Continue With Core Academic Classes: Colleges want to see students take the core academic classes all four years. These include English, math, history, science, and foreign language.

Research College Requirements: Research the specific course requirements for the colleges your student is interested in attending. This will ensure your child is taking the necessary courses to meet those requirements. For example, the University of California schools have a required one-year art course for all applicants, taken from the following disciplines: music, theater, dance, visual arts, or interdisciplinary arts.

Maintain Rigor In Your Classes: AP and dual-enrollment courses are challenging, college-level classes offered in most high schools. These courses can often help students earn college credits while still in high school. Most importantly, students should maintain the same rigor they have had in their three previous years of high school.

Encourage Students To Take A Mix Of Academic And Elective Courses: While it's essential for students to focus on their academic subjects, they should also explore their interests through elective courses. Encourage your student to try a variety of classes to find out what they enjoy and where they excel.

Seek Guidance From School Counselor And Teachers: Your child's school counselor and teachers can provide valuable guidance and support as students plan for college. Encourage your students to seek help as they plan their course schedules.

TIPS

- Students should take challenging courses if they can make good grades and are not stressed by the extra work.
- Students should be prepared with options before they go to register.
- Consider the teachers who are teaching the class.
- Don't let up. Colleges will want to see a continued effort through the entire senior year. Senioritis is a real problem for 2nd-semester seniors.
- **Colleges have the right to rescind a previous acceptance if a student grades significantly drop during their senior year.**

Student Checklist

1. Have you talked with your high school counselor about your schedule?
2. What classes have you signed up for next year?
3. Do you have all of the classes you need to graduate?

Strategy 7

Social Media and Virtual Opportunities: From Likes to Acceptance

Connecting with colleges through social media can provide valuable insights and information to help your student decide where to apply and attend. Colleges and universities often use social media platforms like X, Instagram, LinkedIn, and YouTube to share updates and news about their campus, student life, academic programs, and admissions process.

Follow College Social Media Accounts: Most colleges and universities have social media accounts. By following these accounts, your child can stay up to date with the latest news, events, and announcements from the colleges.

Join Relevant Groups: Many colleges have groups on social media that are specific to different departments, sports, and organizations. Joining these groups and pages can be an excellent way for students to connect with others with similar interests and get involved in college activities.

Participate In Online Groups And Discussions: Many universities now offer virtual events and discussions on social media platforms. Students can participate in these events and conversations to determine whether the school might be a good fit.

Attend Virtual College Fairs: Virtual college fairs are hosted by many colleges, which allow students to connect with admissions representatives and learn about different schools and programs.

Attend Virtual Information Sessions: Frequently, colleges offer virtual information sessions, which are webinars or online presentations that provide an overview of the school and its programs. These sessions often include a Q&A portion, allowing students to ask questions and get more information.

Take Virtual College Tours: If students can't visit in person, visit online. Many colleges offer virtual tours of their campuses, allowing students to explore the campus remotely. These tours can include videos, photos, interactive maps, and information about different buildings, facilities, and amenities.

Email Schools: You can email colleges to ask questions or learn more about their programs. Many colleges have admissions offices or other departments dedicated to helping prospective students.

Create A Linkedin Account: A LinkedIn profile can be a digital resume, allowing your student to showcase their academic achievements, extracurricular activities, and work experience. This can help them build their professional brand and stand out to colleges and potential part-time or summer employers.

Students can use the platform to find and join professional groups and learn new skills through LinkedIn Learning. LinkedIn has a job search feature that students can use to find internships in their field of interest. Students should use LinkedIn to learn more about schools they are interested in and connect with current students, admission officers, and alums.

FYI - How to Create a LinkedIn Account

- Navigate to the LinkedIn sign-up page.
- Enter your first and last name, email address, and the password you'll use. (Note: You must use your name when creating a profile.)
- Click Join Now.
- Complete any additional steps as prompted.
- Encourage your student to keep their LinkedIn profile updated.
- Your student should connect with teachers at their school, parents, students, and colleges with LinkedIn profiles.

Student Checklist

1. Have you attended any virtual information sessions? At what schools?
2. Have you made any connections on LinkedIn?
3. What colleges are you following on social media?

Fun Idea

Take a road trip to visit colleges and universities. This can be a fun way to explore different campuses and better understand what each school offers and explore the surrounding community. Add a few side trips for a little extra adventure.

Strategy 8

College Visits and Interviews: The Value of Personal Experience

College visits are essential for high school students because they allow them to experience the campus and get a feel for the college atmosphere. This can help students determine if the college fits them academically, socially, and culturally. They also allow students to meet with admissions counselors and faculty members, which can help them learn more about the academic programs and organizations.

College visits enable students to feel more confident and prepared for the college application process, as they have firsthand experience with the college and can use this knowledge to tailor their applications and essays accordingly.

Plan Ahead: Families should notify colleges in advance when they plan to visit. Your student should research the colleges beforehand and list specific places they want to see or topics to address during their visit. This will help them make the most of their time on campus.

Schedule A Tour And Information Session: Most colleges offer guided tours of their campus. These tours are usually led by current students and provide an excellent opportunity to get a feel for the campus and ask questions.

Attend A Class: Many colleges allow prospective students to sit in on a class to understand the academic atmosphere. This is an excellent opportunity to experience a typical class and to get a feel for how the professors interact with students.

Talk With Current Students: Current students can provide valuable insight into what it's like to attend a particular college. Try to find time to chat with students to get their perspective on things like access to professors, clubs and activities, the best dorms for first-year students, and campus life.

Explore The Campus And Surrounding Area: Go beyond the school tour. Take time to explore the local community. Check out nearby restaurants, shopping, and entertainment options. Investigate transportation locally as well as to/from the nearest airport. It's essential to understand what life is like in the area.

Request An Interview: Not all schools do interviews, but asking never hurts. Interviews provide a unique opportunity for your student to demonstrate their true personality. They can also help admission officers understand how well a student would fit in with the college's culture and community. Take advantage of the opportunity if available. It can be a very influential factor for college admission. Remember to ask for the interviewer's card and follow up with a thank-you note.

TIPS

- Your student should do a virtual tour before an in-person visit.
- Ensure you and your student document what you like and don't like about a school.
- Take a lot of photos to help remember each school.

Questions to Ask the Tour Guide

- What do you like most about this school?
- How hard is it to get the classes you want each semester?
- What's your biggest complaint about this school?
- What's your best advice for a new freshman?
- What was your most significant adjustment to college?
- What's your favorite activity on campus?
- What dorm do you recommend for first-year students?

Student Checklist

1. Have you made plans to do any college visits?
2. Did you contact admissions to ask about attending a class?
3. Have you emailed any of your colleges about doing an interview?
4. Have you thought about an interview with a professor in your particular area of interest?

Strategy 9

College Fairs: Standing Out from the Crowd

Attending college fairs is an essential part of the college search process. These fairs provide students with the opportunity to meet with representatives from a variety of schools in one location. It's an opportunity for your student to ask questions and gather information directly from college representatives. It can be a valuable resource for making informed decisions about where to apply and attend. Additionally, attending college fairs can help students understand the application process, financial aid options, and other vital aspects of college admissions.

Students Should Research Colleges Before They Attend: Have your child research the colleges that interest them at the fair so they better understand what each school offers and can ask more targeted questions.

Help Students Come Up With A Few Questions To Ask: Encourage your student to think of two or three questions to ask college representatives at the fair. This might include questions about the admissions process, financial aid options, academics, or campus life.

Should Your Student Bring Materials To The Fair?: Some college representatives might ask to see a resume or a high school transcript. This can help your student stand out to college representatives and make it easier for them to follow up after the fair. Some students bring a business card with their name, school, and contact information.

Discuss Appropriate Dress: It is always important to dress in business casual attire for the fair. This will help your student make a good impression on college representatives and show they are serious about their future.

Have Your Students Follow Up: Your student should follow up with the colleges they are interested in after the fair. They can email the college representatives with additional questions or say they enjoyed meeting them at the fair. It's an easy way to stay connected.

TIPS

- Register online for the fair and check the list of participating schools so you know which ones you want to visit.
- Check the floor plan if it is available to find the schools you want to talk to within the two or three-hour limit that most college fairs have.
- Practice your introduction before attending the fair. Always shake hands, make good eye contact, clearly state your first and last name, and be attentive to the college representative.
- Arrive early as some schools will have long waiting lines.
- Ask insightful questions, and be genuine. Stay away from questions that can be answered by a simple Google search or going to the website.

Student Checklist

1. What colleges did you visit at the college fair?
2. Are there any schools that particularly interest you?
3. What college representatives impressed you the most?

Fun Idea

How about a college-themed trivia game with your child? The participants have five minutes to use their phones to look up information about a school. This can be a fun way to learn more about different colleges.

Strategy 10

Teacher Recommendations: Choosing the Right Teachers

It's vital that a teacher can speak to a student's interest. Teacher recommendations are an essential part of the college admission process because they provide insights into your student's academic abilities, character, and potential for success in college.

Admission officers rely on teacher recommendations to gain a more holistic view of applicants beyond their grades and test scores. Moreover, they can provide context for your student's academic performance and demonstrate their potential for success.

Choosing The Right Teachers: Your student should choose teachers who know them well and can speak to their strengths and abilities. Colleges want to see effort, participation, and students exceeding expectations. It's vital that a teacher can speak to the student's interest in their course, their ability to seek help when needed and assist others who need it.

Ask For Recommendations Early: Your student should request recommendations early to give teachers plenty of time. Start by talking with teachers before the end of the spring semester of junior year. Some teachers limit the number of recommendations they will write or respond to them in the requested order.

Provide Teachers With Information: Provide teachers with information about your goals and interests, a copy of your resume, or a list of your extracurricular activities and achievements. This will help teachers write more detailed and personalized recommendations.

Show Appreciation: Your student should appreciate teachers' time and effort in writing recommendations. A handwritten note can go a long way in thanking teachers for their help.

Follow-Up: If students have not heard back from a teacher within a week after requesting a recommendation, following up with a gentle reminder is a good idea. This will help ensure that submissions are completed before a college deadline.

Submitting Recommendations: Students link Naviance or a similar account to their Common Application. Then they request which teachers they want to write recommendations. When the teacher is finished, they upload the submission.

TIPS

- Submitting teacher recommendations is always beneficial, even if a college or university does not require them.
- Colleges want to know how students compare to others in the same class.
- Most colleges want to see recommendations from core class teachers. (English, math, science, history, or foreign language) They also prefer them from junior-year teachers if possible.

Student Checklist

1. Which teachers are you asking for recommendations?
2. Have you met with them and given them your resume?

Strategy 11

Demonstrating Interest: Show Colleges You Care

Demonstrating interest in colleges is an essential aspect of the college application process, as it indicates to admissions officers that you are serious about attending their institution. It also shows a college that you have taken the time to learn more about their school. Showing interest can be an advantage in admissions.

Attend Locally Sponsored Events: Frequently, individual colleges or small groups of colleges will host events in the local area. You and your student need to attend.

Apply To The College: Applying to a college is a straightforward way for your student to show interest in the school. Be sure to complete their application carefully, follow all instructions and pay special attention to the "Why this College?" essay.

Read Your Emails: Many colleges track how often students read their emails, so opening them and clicking links is essential.

Participate In College-Specific Programs: Many colleges offer programs specifically designed for students interested in attending the school. Participating in these programs can be an excellent way for your student to show interest in the school and demonstrate their commitment to attending.

Contact College Representatives: Your student needs to get to know college representatives because they can serve as a valuable resource for information and support during the application process. They can help students navigate the administrative aspects of college life, such as financial aid and housing. They also advocate for your student as they may be the first to read their application. So, start connecting through email at the beginning of your senior year.

FYI - Contacting the College Representative

Below is a template you can use to communicate with college admissions representatives. Keep it formal and to the point.

> Hi COLLEGE REPRESENTATIVE NAME,
>
> I am a GRADE and attend HIGH SCHOOL in CITY, STATE.
>
> I am very interested in NAME OF COLLEGE and would like to ask you a few questions (Choose 2 from the list below)
>
> 1.
>
> 2.
>
> Thank you so much for your time. I look forward to hearing back from you at your earliest convenience.
>
> Sincerely,
>
> YOUR FULL NAME
> MOBILE NUMBER

Questions to Ask a College Representative

- How would you describe your students in three adjectives?
- What conversations are you likely to overhear at your school, but maybe not at other colleges?
- What advice do you have for an incoming student?
- Beyond ranking, GPA, and test scores, what kind of student would thrive and excel at your school?
- Are there different admissions requirements for various departments or majors?
- What academic, mental health, or other support is offered for first-year students?
- What are the undergraduate opportunities for internships, research, and employment?

Student Checklist

1. Have you contacted the college representatives at the schools that interest you?
2. Have you checked your email today? What colleges have contacted you?

Strategy 12

Narrowing Down the College List: From Many to Few(er)

The revised college list should be a balanced mix of reach, target and probable schools. Typically, students should have two or three reach schools, three target and three or four probable. You want your student to have choices when it comes to making their college decision.

- **Reach Schools:** These are colleges where the student's chances of admission are considered unlikely. These are typically highly competitive and prestigious institutions that have a low acceptance rate. Students may have strong academic credentials, but that is often not enough. These are schools that usually accept less than 30% of their applicants.
- **Target Schools:** These are colleges where a student's academic profile, GPA, standardized test scores, and extracurricular involvement falls within the typical range of admitted students. While admission is not guaranteed, students have a reasonably good chance of being accepted

based on their qualifications. These are schools that usually accept somewhere between 30% and 60% of their applicants.

- **Probable schools:** These are colleges where the student's academic profile exceeds the typical qualifications of admitted students. These institutions are considered less competitive, and students have a higher probability of being admitted. These are usually schools that accept 60% or more of their applicants

Narrowing the List: After each school has been thoroughly researched, college visits (virtual or in person) have been taken and your student has attended an information session, it may be time to narrow down the college list. This process requires students to pare down their list of schools to those that best match their needs, interests, and family finances.

Eliminating Schools: What colleges do not meet the priorities your student wants in a school? Make a shortlist of colleges that appeal to them based on what is most important in a college experience. The list should include eight or nine schools in total.

No Need to Rush: Students should not be in a hurry to narrow down their college list. This can happen anytime during the application process. They should aim to have a final list of colleges that they would be happy to attend and that meet their priorities and goals.

FYI - Three Types of College Applications

- **Common Application:** The Common Application is a standardized application that allows students to apply to over 1,000 colleges and universities with a single application. The Common App includes sections for personal information, academic history, extracurricular activities, and essays.

- **Coalition Application:** The Coalition Application is another standardized application that allows students to apply to over 140 colleges and universities. Like the Common App, the Coalition App includes sections for personal information, academic history, extracurricular activities, essays, and a resume.
- **School Specific Application:** Some colleges and universities have specific application forms that students must use to apply. These applications will be available online at each school's website.

By understanding the different types of college applications, your student can choose the option that best fits their needs and apply to the colleges that interest them.

Student Checklist

1. Could you be happy at every school on your list?
2. Are you sure your list is balanced?
3. Are you interested in taking any colleges off your list and adding others in their place?

Strategy 13

The Power of Personalization: Making Your Application Unique

A standout college application is essential because it can differentiate your student from the thousands of other applicants vying for admission to a particular college or university. It can also show the admissions committee that the applicant has taken the time and effort to craft a thoughtful and comprehensive application, indicating their interest level and why they would be a good fit for the college.

Research Schools: Your college application needs to show that you are familiar with each school and how it might be a potential fit for you. This requires research and getting to know the college so that students understand the school's mission and specifics as to what it offers.

Encourage Students To Focus On Their Strengths: Your child should identify and highlight their strengths in their applications. This might include their academic achievements, extracurricular activities, and personal interests. Colleges want to know how an applicant will impact the school now, and in the future.

Help Students Craft A Compelling Personal Statement: The personal statement is an integral part of the college application, it's a chance for students to showcase their personality and writing skills. **The first paragraph needs to catch the reader's attention!**

Strong Letters Of Recommendation: Letters of recommendation from teachers, counselors, and other individuals who know your student well can help bolster their college application. Encourage your student to request letters of recommendation from teachers and counselors who speak to their strengths and accomplishments.

Spend Time On Supplemental Essays: Some college admission officers indicate that supplemental essays can be significant in determining whether a student is a good fit. When a school's essay prompt asks you why you want to go there, use specific details like programs, organizations, and courses of interest to you at that school. Be specific!

Proofread The Applications: Students should proofread their applications carefully. This involves a final check for spelling, punctuation, grammar, repeated words, omitted words, spacing, and typographical errors.

TIPS

- The activity section should describe your involvement, not the activity itself.
- Many colleges report they consider character of importance in their college applicants. Do your student's applications and essays demonstrate positive character traits?
- AXS Companion is a free, online resource to be used with the Common Application as students work through their application.

FYI - Different College Deadlines

There are different application deadline options for colleges including early action, restricted early action, early decision, early decision II and rolling admissions are all different application deadline options for college. Students need to understand the implications of each before they send their college applications. Some schools offer each of these options, and others may not.

Early Action: With early action, students can apply to a college early and receive a decision earlier than regular admission candidates. However, unlike early decision, students are not required to commit to attending the college if accepted. They can continue to apply to other colleges and compare financial aid offers before making a final decision. Early action shows a school that a student is interested and organized. Many believe that it can slightly improve a student's chances for admission.

Restricted Early Action (REA): Restricted Early Action is a modified version of early action. Some colleges and universities offer it, allowing students to apply early and receive an admission decision ahead of the regular application pool. However, unlike regular early action, REA usually has restrictions, such as limiting students from applying to other private institutions under an early plan (early decision or early action) and requiring them to refrain from submitting additional applications until they receive a decision.

Early Decision: With early decision, students apply to one college and agree to attend if accepted. This is a binding commitment, so students cannot apply to other colleges through early decision. By using early decision, students limit their options if they are not accepted or receive a better financial aid package from another school. Early-decision applicants usually have a better chance of being accepted to their first-choice college as they demonstrate a solid commitment to the school. Almost all colleges will let early-decision applicants know their decision sometime in December.

Early Decision II (ED II): Early Decision II is the second round of the Early Decision program some schools offer. It operates similarly to Early Decision, where students apply early and receive an admission decision ahead of the regular application pool. However, ED II has a later application deadline than the standard Early Decision round, usually in January or February. It gives students who missed the early deadlines or need more time to decide an opportunity to apply early and still be bound by the commitment to attend the institution if accepted.

Rolling Admissions: With rolling admissions, colleges review applications as they are received and notify applicants of their decision on a rolling basis rather than waiting until a specific deadline. This means that applicants may receive a decision earlier than regular admission candidates. Still, they may also have to wait longer if they apply later. Rolling admissions may be a good option for students still deciding on their college plans or needing more time to complete their applications.

It's essential to consider the pros and cons of each of these options before deciding which one is right for you. Early decision can be a good choice for students confident in their ability to be accepted to their first-choice college and sure that it is where they want to attend. Still, there may be better options if you are still determining your college plans or want to compare financial aid offers from multiple schools.

Student Checklist

1. Do you know all your application deadlines?
2. Have you decided to apply to any schools early action?
3. Have you described your activities as clearly as possible?

Strategy 14

Brainstorming College Essay Topics: Generating Winning Ideas

Brainstorming ideas is crucial for a college admission essay because it allows your student to explore their thoughts and ideas freely and comc up with unique and compelling stories that showcase their personality, experiences, and strengths.

Consider Potential Topics: Students should start by listing potential essay topics. They can write down anything that comes to mind, even if it seems silly or unimportant. The goal is to generate as many ideas as possible.

Reflect On Personal Experiences: One effective way to brainstorm is to reflect on personal experiences that have been meaningful or transformative. These experiences can be from any aspect of your student's life, such as a significant event, an influential person, or an important interest.

Use Prompts: College essay prompts are available online, and students can use them as a starting point for brainstorming ideas. Even if the prompt does not directly relate to the student's experience, it can still be a helpful tool to inspire ideas.

Solicit Feedback: After brainstorming some ideas, your student should share them with a family member or mentor. Getting feedback can provide a new perspective and help your student refine their ideas.

Consider The Essay's Purpose: It's important to remember that the college admission essay aims to showcase the student's personality, values, and experiences. Therefore, students should choose topics that allow them to demonstrate these qualities and stand out.

Help Students Think Creatively: Encourage them to come up with unique ideas for the topics they have selected and the approach they want to take.

Think About Values And Goals: What are your child's values and goals? How have they influenced their choices and decisions in the past? Students can show character in a college essay by sharing stories demonstrating the strengths and challenges they have overcome. They can convey their personality, passion, and authenticity through their writing.

Consider Unique Qualities: Students must consider what makes them unique and special. What sets them apart from other applicants?

Narrow-Down Ideas: From the list they have brainstormed, students should choose the topic they feel most passionate about, showcasing their personality and who they genuinely are.

TIPS

- Some schools will have optional, not supplemental, essays on their application.
- Some colleges pay more attention to supplemental essays than the main essay.

- Short answer essays can tell a school a lot about your student. They should receive as much attention as the more extended main essay.

Student Checklist

1. What topics did you consider for your Common App essay?
2. Why did you choose the topic you did?
3. Does your essay topic distinguish you from other applicants?

Strategy 15

Crafting A College Essay: Making It Memorable

To write an outstanding college essay, it is essential to understand what the admissions committee is looking for in an applicant. The essay should be well organized, with a strong thesis statement and clear supporting evidence. It should also be engaging and well-written, with a compelling opening and a memorable conclusion. Students should write an essay that sets them apart from other applicants.

Start Early: Get your student to write their essay during the summer before their senior year. This will give them ample time to brainstorm, write, and revise their essay before school starts.

Use A Strong Introduction: Get the reader's attention with a descriptive anecdote, question or insightful statement that will make your reader want to read more.

Do Not Try To Impress: The Common Application essay should be personal and meaningful to your student. Encourage them to consider their experiences, values, and goals.

Be Authentic: Encourage your student to be authentic and honest in their writing. The admissions committee wants to get to know the actual student, so they need to be sincere in their writing. This can also help make their essays more engaging.

Be Specific: Your child should use specific examples and anecdotes in their essay to illustrate their points and bring their story to life. This will help the admissions committee understand who they are and what they care about.

Be Vulnerable: This can help students connect with the reader and make their essays more compelling. Showing a sensitive side is positive!

Write A Rough Draft: Students must start with a rough essay draft. This will help them organize their thoughts and better understand the direction they want their essay to take. Most students write multiple drafts.

Set Aside The Essay For A Few Days: Revising the essay with fresh eyes after taking a break can help students find areas that might need improvement. Students should limit outside opinions to a few trusted people. Getting too many opinions can make them question their topic and the writing and cause additional stress.

Edit And Revise: Encourage your student to edit and revise their essay carefully. They should proofread for grammar and spelling errors. Most importantly, they need to make every word count!

Follow The Rules: The Common Application essay should be no longer than 650 words. Students should stay somewhere around 550 - 600 words. The application will cut the essay off if it exceeds the word limit.

TIPS

- Avoid repeating information that is already on the application. Refrain from rehashing your extracurricular or academic accomplishments.
- Consider a way to take your topic and offer a unique perspective.
- Have your student read their essay aloud. They will hear awkward sentences, overuse of certain words and transitions that don't sound smooth.
- Some students will want to share their essay with you, and some won't. Don't be offended if they choose not to!

FYI - The Common Application Optional Essay

The Common Application additional section is optional, allowing students to add additional information that may not be covered elsewhere in their application. This section can include the following information:

- Extenuating circumstances not mentioned in any other part of the application.
- Discrepancies in the application.
- Links to a portfolio, research project, or website that belongs to them
- Unusual educational history - Moving and changing schools numerous times.
- Changes in family circumstances.

Student Checklist

1. Read the first paragraph of your essay. Does it get your reader's attention?
2. What does your essay tell about you?
3. Have you proofread it to make sure it is error free?

Fun Idea

Have a college-themed cooking night. Cook a meal with your child that a college or university inspires. For example, you could make a pizza inspired by the University of Michigan's famous "pizza house." This can be a fun way to learn unusual or interesting facts about the colleges on your student's shortlist and incorporate them into your daily life.

Strategy 16

Paying for College: Breaking the Tuition Barrier

Making college affordable is a goal many families share as the cost of higher education rises. Paying for college can be a significant financial burden for families, so it is essential to start saving as early as possible. Discussing with your teen what you are willing and able to pay for college is important. Families must explore their financial options so students only take on debt that is necessary.

Search Online: Some online databases and websites offer information about college scholarships, such as Fastweb, Scholarships.com, and College Board. These resources can be a great starting point for students looking for scholarships.

Be aware, however, that many scholarship websites take students' information and use it for spam.

Check With The Colleges: Most colleges and universities are applicants' best scholarship sources. Students should check with the financial aid office at the colleges they are interested in.

Look For Scholarships From Local Organizations And Foundations: Students can also look for scholarships from organizations and foundations that align with their interests or goals. For example, students interested in science may be able to find scholarships from science-based organizations. Rotary, Elks, religious organizations, and parents' employer are good sources to try. Students can search for professional organizations by entering their city's name and foundations into a search engine and phrases like "professional association" to find local chapters.

Ask For Help: Students can find scholarships from their school counselor, who can point them to resources and opportunities they may have not considered before. Check the college counseling websites at nearby high schools for potential scholarships.

Be Proactive: Students should be proactive in their search for scholarships. This may involve contacting organizations and foundations directly or networking with individuals who can help them find scholarship opportunities.

Local scholarships are less competitive than state or national scholarships, and the application process is not as complex.

Start Early And Watch Deadlines: Students should apply for as many scholarships as possible to increase their chances of receiving money for college. It's important to carefully follow each scholarship's application instructions and deadlines to ensure that entries are considered.

Complete The FAFSA (Free Application For Federal Student Aid) When It Becomes Available Online: The FAFSA is required for students to qualify for financial aid. Fill out the CSS profile in addition, if your student is applying to private schools where it is required.

FYI - Sources of Financial Aid

- **Grants:** Grants are financial aid that does not have to be repaid. They are typically based on financial need and may be awarded by the federal government, state government, or the college itself. Examples include the Federal Pell Grant, the Federal Supplemental Educational Opportunity Grant (FSEOG), and state-based grants.
- **Scholarships:** Scholarships are financial aid based on merit rather than financial need. They may come from the college, a private organization, or a community group and do not need to be repaid.
- **Loans:** Loans are financial aid that must be repaid with interest. There are two main types of loans: federal student loans, which the federal government offers, and private student loans, which banks and other lenders provide. Federal student loans generally have lower interest rates and more flexible repayment terms than private student loans.
- **Work-Study:** A federal financial aid program allows students to work part-time on campus or in a related field to earn money to help pay for college expenses.
- **Additional Sources:** Consider starting a Roth IRA, investing in mutual funds or taking out a home equity loan.

It's essential to consider the terms and conditions of any financial aid you receive, as it may affect your future financial obligations. Exploring multiple sources of financial aid may also help you find the best options to meet your needs.

TIPS

- Many families invest in a 529 college saving program, a tax-advantaged savings plan designed to encourage saving for future education expenses.
- Always take advantage of low-interest federal student loans first.
- Going to college in-state is only sometimes the best financial decision. Some in-state schools still have high tuition comparatively. Some out-of-state colleges offer merit scholarships that make an in-state school more expensive.
- Small loans are something that many students will need to attend college, but students should have no more debt than is absolutely necessary. Choose schools with the least amount of debt.
- Always use the net price calculator on college websites to get an idea of the expected family contribution for the colleges on a student's list.
- Filling out the FAFSA makes sense for every family. If circumstances change, you might be very thankful you did!
- Ask colleges about installment plans and guaranteed cost plans.
- Check your state's financial aid programs.
- If parents are divorced, choose the financial information from the parent with the lower income. If a parent has remarried, this could be a stepparent.

FYI - Merit Scholarships

Merit scholarships are awards given to students based on academic, athletic, or artistic merit rather than financial need. Colleges and universities often offer these scholarships to attract top students to their schools.

There are several steps that students can follow to find and apply for college scholarships:

Identify Your Goals: Students should consider what they want to study, where they want to go to college, and what they hope to do after graduation. This will help them focus their scholarship search on relevant opportunities.

Research Scholarship Options: Many resources are available to help applicants find scholarships, including their high school counselor, the financial aid office at the colleges they are considering, and online scholarship databases.

Get Organized: Students should list the scholarships they are interested in and their deadlines. Then they must keep track of any required materials, such as transcripts, recommendation letters, and essays.

Tailor Your Application: Students should carefully read the requirements for each scholarship they apply for and tailor the application to meet those requirements.

Submitting Your Application: Carefully review scholarship applications before submitting and follow any instructions provided. Be sure to submit applications by the deadlines.

Follow-Up: If students do not hear back from the scholarship committee, follow up with a polite email or phone call to inquire about the status of the application.

TIPS

- Students should always look for merit scholarships on a college website.
- Merit scholarships do not need to be repaid.
- **Always check the requirements for a merit scholarship. For example, is there a minimum GPA that students need to maintain each semester in order to keep the scholarship?**
- Pay attention to the scholarship's guidelines. To keep your scholarship money, check your school's policies about stacking. For example, there may be scholarships A, B, and C, where the student can get only the largest of the ones that they earn, but there may be other scholarships X, Y, and Z that may be stacked on any of A, B, and C or each other. Each school is different on their stacking policy.
- Check out this website that matches your student with potential merit scholarships: meritmore.com
- Some colleges do not require a separate scholarship application, but some do. Check dates for scholarship applications and get them in on time, or earlier than the stated deadline.

Student Checklist

1. What college websites have you examined to see if you qualify for merit awards?
2. Have you inquired or applied for any local scholarships?

3. What scholarships do your colleges offer?
4. Have you checked your high school counseling office for scholarships?
5. How can you contribute financially to your college education?
6. How can you contribute financially to your college education?

Strategy 17

What if Financial Aid and Scholarships Are Not Enough?

Sometimes financial aid and scholarships are not sufficient to cover the costs of attending college. The key is to be proactive and persistent in your efforts. It's essential to remember that financial aid offers are typically based on funds and the school's policies, and it may not always be possible to get an increase in aid. However, it is always worth reaching out to the financial aid office and explaining the student's situation to secure additional assistance.

First, there are a few things you should do:

Understand The Components Of The Financial Aid Package: This includes grants, scholarships, loans, and work-study opportunities. Pay particular attention to the loans!

Research The Cost Of Attending At Each School: This includes tuition and fees, as well as other expenses such as housing, transportation, Greek life, insurance and books.

Contact The Financial Aid Office At A School And Explain The Student's Situation: Be prepared to provide documentation to support the applicant's request for additional aid. Be specific in naming a number that will help the student bridge the gap needed to attend the school. For example, "$5000 more would make a big difference."

Ask For A Review Of The Financial Aid Package: Be specific about what the student is requesting. For example, they might ask for an increase in grants or scholarships or a reduction in the loan amount offered. Consider appealing to other sources of financial aid, such as private scholarships or external assistance. You can always inquire about additional federal loans that may be available.

Make Your Case: If your child feels they deserve more financial aid, make a case for it. Explain their financial need, academic achievements, and other factors that make your child a good candidate for additional aid. Also, if your student has received more financial aid from a similar school, it may be worth a mention as long as the documentation is available.

TIPS

- Call colleges if your family's financial circumstances have changed.
- Don't use the word negotiate; use discuss or petition instead.

Student Checklist

1. Do you understand your financial aid package from every school?
2. Have you looked into a Federal work-study program?
3. Are there any departmental (major-specific) scholarships available for you?

Strategy 18

Making the Final Decision: From Pros and Cons to the Ultimate Choice

Ultimately, you want your student to make the final decision, but it's your role as a parent to help them consider their options and support and guide them through the process. No school will be perfect, but hopefully students will choose one that is right for them!

Review Acceptance Letters: If your student has applied to multiple colleges, they should review all the acceptance letters and compare the offers from each school. Your students should consider location, cost, academic programs, campus culture, and overall fit. They should also connect with the schools to get answers to any questions they might have.

Help Your Student Create A List Of Pros And Cons: Encourage your student to list the pros and cons of each college they are considering. This can help them weigh the different factors and make a more informed decision.

Consider The Cost: Families must discuss whether they can afford the colleges their child has chosen. Students and parents should not take on any more debt than necessary. While this may be difficult for your student to understand, they will appreciate it later.

Is Another College Visit Necessary?: Sometimes, students need to visit the campus of their top choice colleges again to see how they feel about the campus environment. This can help them decide whether they can see themselves at this school for the next four years.

TIPS - Things to Keep in Mind

- Your student must commit to a college or university by May 1st.
- Remind your student that what they do at a university is far more important than the school's name or rank.
- Your student needs to notify the other colleges to which they have been accepted to let them know they will not be attending. This opens a spot for someone who has been waitlisted.
- Sometimes, flipping a coin can be very telling. If it is heads, it is one school, tails another. Watch your student's reaction as they flip the coin and it lands. Are they disappointed or do they seem pleased with the decision?
- Often, students know themselves best. Suggest they go with their gut feeling in making a decision.

Student Checklist

1. Have you reconsidered your priorities for your college experience?
2. How does cost factor into your decision?
3. Have you weighed up the pros and cons of every school?

Fun Idea

Enjoy a final decision party. Buy some college pennants or flags, a sweatshirt, and a baseball cap from the school your student will be attending. Serve your teen's favorite dinner and have a party for your family to celebrate!

Strategy 19

After the Final Decision:
Moving On with Confidence

Congratulations! The decision has been made to attend your college for the next chapter of your academic journey. This marks a significant milestone in your life, but it's essential to remember that your work doesn't end here. So, let's dive in and explore what comes next after committing to your school.

Accept An Offer Of Admission: All colleges formally require students to accept their offer of admission by May 1st. This typically involves paying a deposit and completing any necessary paperwork. Your student is only allowed to make a deposit at one school.

Request Final Transcripts And Test Scores: Most colleges will require students to submit their final transcripts and test scores as part of enrollment. Be sure to check with the admissions office to find out what documentation is required. Students must request transcripts from their high school counseling office, and official test scores should be sent directly from the College Board or ACT.

Sign Up For Campus Housing: If students live on campus, they must sign up for housing. This typically involves completing a housing application and paying a deposit. Students often join online groups of accepted students at their school and get to know others who might be potential roommates. Some colleges provide roommate matching services which students sign up for. **Housing deposits are usually non-refundable!**

Register For Student Orientation: Most colleges offer new student orientation programs to help students acclimate to campus life. It is essential to attend these programs to learn about the school's resources and meet other new students. Your student will usually register for the first semester classes during orientation.

Set Up A Student Account: Your student must set up a student account to access their academic records and other resources. This usually involves creating a login and password. Information will be sent to you once you commit to a school.

Make Doctor Appointments: Book a doctor's appointment and have the necessary vaccinations, a physical exam, and health forms signed. Also, schedule a dentist appointment and one with the ophthalmologist if your child wears glasses or contacts.

By following these steps, you can ensure that your child will be prepared to start college and have a smooth transition to campus life.

FYI - Legal Documents for Students

- FERPA Release Form-Gives parents access to educational records
- HIPPA-Allows doctors to share medical information
- Medical Power of Attorney-Allows parents to make medical decisions

- Get your Young Adult Power of Attorney Package online. The website Mama Bear provides law-firm quality, state-specific documents that you can download and use.

Student Checklist

1. Did you make a housing deposit?
2. Have you signed up for freshmen orientation?
3. Have you requested your final transcript be sent to the college you are attending?

Strategy 20

Transitioning to College: Moving from Home to Campus

Transitioning from high school to college is an exciting, but challenging journey. This period of change is an opportunity for independence, exploration and personal growth, but it can also be filled with uncertainties. Whether you're feeling excited, anxious, or a mix of both, there are strategies to navigate the adventure and discover the keys to thriving in your new college environment.

Start Getting Organized Early: College is a big transition; being organized can help students stay on track and feel more in control. Encourage them to start by setting up a schedule for their classes, homework, campus activities, exercise and relaxation. They should also find a study space that works for them. Some students find it difficult to study in the dorm and prefer going to the library or another location that may be quieter.

Setting Goals: College is a great time for students to start thinking about their long-term goals, both academic and personal. Encourage students to set goals for themselves and work towards them consistently. Be a good listener, but allow your student to be in charge.

Take Care Of Themselves: College is also a time for students to learn how to take care of themselves physically and mentally. Encourage students to eat well, exercise, get enough sleep, and take breaks when needed.

Seek Out Support: College can sometimes be overwhelming, and students need a support system they can rely on. Encourage students to contact their professors, academic advisors, or counselors if they need help. Meeting with a professor, advisor or mentor can help keep students on track with graduation requirements and graduate in four years. Students should also take advantage of professors' office hours so the professor can get to know them.

Stay Connected: Students should stay connected with their family and friends from home. This can help them feel more supported and grounded as they navigate the challenges of college life. However, it is also wise to warn students that what they see on social media from their friends may not be realistic because often students only post when they are having a good time.

Encourage Independence: Encourage students to be independent. As much as parents may want to help their children, they need to allow them to take charge. Even if students don't want help, parents can still listen and be available to assist. Parents need to trust their children's judgment and allow them to make their own decisions. Students should find solutions to problems independently before they come to a parent for help. Advise them first to utilize the college resources that are available.

Suggest Your Student Gets Involved: Participating in community service activities, intramural sports, and campus organizations can help students build leadership skills, make new friends, and explore their interests. This will also help them feel part of the campus community, making the college transition much easier.

Discuss The Importance Of Good Grades: Good grades are important for maintaining financial aid and scholarships. It is also easier to start off with a semester of good grades than it is to dig yourself out from a bad semester. Encourage your student to work hard and do their best work.

Student Checklist

1. What environment is best for you to study?
2. Have you found any activities that interest you?
3. Are you comfortable with the transition to college?
4. Do you have strategies to set yourself up for success?

Admission Scenarios

Waitlisted Students

Waitlisted students have yet to be accepted or rejected by a particular college or university. If space becomes available, they may be offered admission, but there are no guarantees.

Encourage your students to stay positive. It can be frustrating and disappointing to be waitlisted, but the student needs to remain optimistic and keep their options open. Help them to stay focused on their goals and encourage them to keep working hard.

Make a Plan: Encourage your student to plan what they will do if they are not accepted off the waitlist.

Your Student Should Stay In Touch With The College: If your student is interested in attending the college, encourage them to stay in touch with the admissions office. They can send additional materials, such as updated transcripts or recommendation letters, to show their continued interest in the school.

TIPS

- Students should not wait until the end of June to hear whether they have been accepted off the waitlist. A student needs time to commit to one school, start looking for a roommate, and get excited about attending.

- Frequently, students taken off the waitlist are full pay and need no financial aid.
- Students often come off the waitlist because they fulfill an institutional need that the college has: athlete, musician, geography, first-generation, etc.

Deferred Students

If a student is deferred from a college, the college has decided to postpone deciding on the student's application until later. This can be a frustrating and stressful experience for your student, as it means they will have to wait longer to find out if they have been accepted to the college. However, there are a few things that your student can do if they are deferred:

Understand The Reason For The Deferral: If your student is deferred from a college, they need to understand the reason. Your college representative might be able to help you. Some colleges defer students because they want to see how the student performs in the second semester of their senior year. In contrast, others defer students because they are still considering many applicants. Understanding the reason for the deferral can help students work to strengthen their application.

Update The College On Any New Achievements: If your student has made significant academic or extracurricular achievements since submitting their application, they should update the college on these achievements. This can help the college see that your student is still actively engaged and motivated and may strengthen their case for acceptance.

Consider Applying To Additional Colleges: While it can be disappointing to be deferred from a college, students must remember that there are many other great colleges and universities. Students who are deferred should consider applying to other colleges in case their initial first choice does not work out.

Keep In Touch With The College: Students deferred from a college should contact the admissions office to express their continued interest in attending the school. This can be done through a phone call, email, or handwritten letter. Keeping in touch with the college helps the admissions office remember the student's application and may increase your student's chances of being accepted later.

TIPS

- Students who are deferred still have a chance of being accepted.
- Deferred students are often accepted after May 1st, when colleges know their yield for their first-year class.

Rejected Students

Validate Their Feelings: It is natural for students to feel upset, frustrated, and even devastated when they are rejected from a college they thought was their "dream" school. It is essential to validate these feelings and let the student know it is okay to feel this way.

Help Them Look At The Bigger Picture: While it can be easy for students to focus on rejection, it is vital to help them look at the bigger picture and remember that there are many other great colleges and universities. Encourage your student to consider different options and apply to other schools.

Encourage Students To Take Care Of Themselves: Dealing with college rejection can be emotionally and mentally draining, so encouraging students to care for themselves is essential. This may include getting enough sleep, eating well, and participating in activities to distract from the rejection.

Help Them Stay Positive: Encourage students to focus on their strengths and accomplishments and remind them that college rejection does not define them. Help your student remain positive and remember that they will eventually find a college that fits them best.

Offer Support: Finally, offering the students ongoing support and encouragement is vital as they navigate the college application process. Let the student know that you are there for them and will support them no matter what.

Help students understand that sometimes institutional needs may lead to college rejection. Colleges and universities may need more students in an under-enrolled major, to play the violin in the orchestra or first-generation students. Students have no control over these institutional needs, and they change from year to year.

Special Circumstances

Learning Disabled Students

Meet With The School Counselor Or Learning Disabilities Specialist: A school counselor or learning specialist can help students understand their learning disability and how it may impact their college experience. They can also help your student develop strategies for managing their disability and accessing accommodations.

Research Colleges And Universities: Look for colleges and universities with programs and support services for students with learning disabilities. Some schools have specialized programs or departments, while others offer a range of accommodations such as extended time for tests or access to assistive technology.

Take College Prep Courses: College preparatory courses can help your student develop the skills and knowledge they need to be successful in college. These courses also help your student become more familiar with the demands of college coursework.

Consider Participating In A Transition Program: Some colleges and universities offer transition programs for students with learning disabilities. These programs can help your student adjust to college life and learn how to access accommodations and support services.

Meet With The Disability Service Office: Once your student has been accepted to a college or university, they should meet with the disability services office to discuss their needs and any accommodations they may require.

Reach Out To Professors And Instructors: If your student requires accommodations in their classes, they should contact their professors and instructors to discuss their needs. This can help ensure your student has the support they need to succeed in their coursework.

Performing Arts Students

Preparing for college as a performing arts student requires a combination of dedication, skill development, and thorough research. Here are some essential steps to help you prepare:

Research Colleges: Begin by researching colleges with strong performing arts programs. Look for institutions that align with your artistic interests, offer the right degree programs (e.g., theater, dance, music, etc.), have renowned faculty members, and provide performance opportunities.

Build Your Portfolio: Develop a portfolio showcasing your talent and experience. Include video clips of performances, photographs, any awards or recognitions, and a resume outlining your training and achievements.

Join Performance Groups: Participate in dance ensembles, local theater productions, or music groups to gain performance experience.

Take Classes and Workshops: Continue your training by taking classes and workshops in your chosen field. Look for local community theaters, dance studios, or music schools that offer programs that can enhance your skills.

Seek Feedback and Coaching: Obtain feedback from teachers, mentors, or industry professionals to identify areas of improvement. Consider private coaching to work on specific techniques or styles.

Prepare Audition Materials: If the college you're applying to requires an audition, prepare your audition materials well in advance. Choose pieces that showcase your strengths and demonstrate versatility.

Practice Regularly: Dedicate time each day to practice and refine your skills. Consistency is key to making progress as a performing artist.

Request Recommendation Letters: Reach out to teachers, mentors, or directors who can provide compelling recommendation letters highlighting your talent, work ethic, and passion for the performing arts.

Student-Athletes

Research Colleges And Athletic Programs: Students should research colleges with strong athletic programs in their sport that align with their academic and personal goals. This may involve looking at the level of competition, coaching staff, facilities, and other factors.

Create A List Of Colleges To Consider: Once the student has identified a few colleges that are a good fit, help them create a list of these colleges and use it to track their progress as they research and apply to each school. Each school on the list should be one that the student would be happy to attend, whether they play their sport or not.

Speak With Coaches: Many college coaches are happy to speak with prospective student-athletes and provide information about their programs. Encourage the student to contact coaches and ask questions about the team, the coaching style, and what they are looking for in recruits.

Create A Recruiting Profile: Many college coaches use recruiting websites to find and evaluate potential recruits. Encourage students to create a recruiting profile on these websites and include information about their athletic and academic achievements and highlights from their games, meets or competitions.

Consider Attending College Showcases And Camps: College showcases and camps are events where student-athletes can showcase their skills and get noticed by college coaches. Encourage your student to attend these events and take advantage of the opportunity to be seen by coaches from various colleges.

Understand The NCAA Eligibility Requirements: Student-athletes need to meet specific academic and amateurism requirements to be eligible to compete in NCAA athletics. Help your student understand these requirements and ensure they meet them as they progress through high school.

It's important to remember that the college recruitment process can be extremely competitive, and it may take time and effort for a student-athlete to find the right fit. Encourage students to be proactive, reach out to coaches and colleges, and keep an open mind as they explore their options.

Students With Mental Health Issues

Encourage Students To Seek Professional Help: If your student is currently receiving treatment for a mental health condition, it's essential to encourage them to continue that treatment when they start college. This may include finding a therapist or counselor on campus or nearby.

Help The Students Create A Plan: Encourage them to develop a plan for managing their mental health in college. This may include setting up regular appointments with a therapist, identifying coping mechanisms and triggers, and creating a support system of friends, family members, and campus resources.

Connect Students With Campus Resources: Many colleges and universities have resources for students with mental health issues, such as counseling centers and student support groups. Help your student connect with these resources to access the support they need.

Discuss The Possibility Of Accommodations: Make sure that your student's mental health condition does not impact their ability to participate in the academic or residential aspects of college. The college disability office may provide extra services to help students succeed.

Educate Your Student About Self-Care: Encourage your student to prioritize self-care and understand that taking care of their mental health is not selfish.

Communicate With Your Student: Keep the lines of communication open and check in on them regularly to see how they're adjusting to college life. Let them know that they can come to you if they need support.

Gap Year

During a gap year, students often explore different areas of interest, gain new experiences, and broaden their horizons. The most common motivations for taking a gap year include personal growth, self-discovery, acquiring new skills, traveling, volunteering, and gaining work experience. Most gap years are at least a semester or two.

Here are some common activities students engage in during their gap year:

- **Traveling:** Many students use a gap year as an opportunity to explore different countries, cultures, and lifestyles. They may backpack through multiple destinations, participate in organized travel programs, or take part in cultural exchange programs.
- **Volunteering:** Gap year participants often dedicate their time to volunteering for various causes, such as environmental conservation, community development, healthcare, education, or humanitarian aid. This allows them to contribute to society while gaining valuable experiences.
- **Work Experience:** Some students choose to work during their gap year to gain practical skills, earn money, or explore potential career paths. They may take on internships, part-time jobs, or even start their own entrepreneurial ventures.
- **Language Learning:** Many students use their gap year to immerse themselves in a foreign language and culture. They may enroll in language courses or live in a country where the language they wish to learn is spoken.
- **Skill Development:** Gap years provide an opportunity to learn practical skills that may not be covered in a formal education setting. Examples include cooking, coding, photography, woodworking, or any skill that interests the student.
- **Cultural Immersion:** Immersing oneself in a different culture can be an enriching experience. Students may choose to live with host families, engage with local communities, participate in cultural festivals, or learn traditional art forms during their gap year.

The concept of a gap year may vary across different countries and cultures. Some educational institutions and employers highly value the experiences gained during a well-structured gap year, recognizing the benefits of increased maturity, independence, and broadened perspectives. However, it's important to consider individual circumstances, such as academic or career goals, financial implications, and potential impact on future plans, before deciding to take a gap year.

Closing Thoughts

As a parent, you play a key role in helping your child navigate the college admission process. This is a significant milestone in the lives of many teenagers, and it presents both opportunities and challenges for them and their parents. This process, can be seen as transitioning from childhood to adulthood, requiring teenagers to make important decisions about their future education and career paths.

As a parent, it is essential to recognize that this process is not just about getting into a good college but also helping your teen find their unique life path. This requires fostering a sense of self-awareness and self-discovery, encouraging your child to explore their passions and interests, and empowering them to make their own decisions. At the same time, we must also provide support and guidance as they navigate the complexities of the college admission process, recognizing that this is a joint effort between parents and children.

As a parent, remember that you are your child's biggest advocate and support system, and by guiding them through the college admission process, you are setting them on a path toward a bright future filled with endless possibilities.

Finally, I want to thank you the reader, for coming along on this college planning journey. I hope you found it beneficial. If so, please take a moment and post a review and tell a friend.

Made in United States
Troutdale, OR
11/11/2023